the Student Voice

Creative Liturgical Design in Schools

Edward Thornley
Chaplain to St Patrick's Episcopal Day School,
Washington DC, USA

GROVE BOOKS LIMITED
RIDLEY HALL RD CAMBRIDGE CB3 9HU

Contents

Acknowledgments

This small book is offered with enormous gratitude to: the parishes and schools of The Dereham and District Team Ministry, Norfolk, UK; The St Marylebone CE School, The St Marylebone CE Bridge School and St Marylebone Parish Church, London, UK; Trinity School, New York, USA; and All Saints' Episcopal School, Fort Worth, Texas, USA.

Anglican Association of Directors of Education

First Impression January 2021
ISSN 2041-0964
ISBN 978 1 78827 150 9

1 Showing Up

> The one who calls you is faithful, and he will do this.
>
> 1 Thess 5.24[1]
>
> You'll never know what a difference you made by just showing up.
>
> A parish priest, Cambridge, 2009

You Will Never Know What Difference You Made...

For five years, I served as the assistant priest in a busy central London parish. Alongside my parish responsibilities, I ministered as chaplain to an all girls' Church of England secondary school and co-educational Sixth Form. In my final year at the school, I was granted the opportunity to develop a new prayer room at the Sixth Form campus.

The room I was given was a small office. Previously, it had been a 'quiet room,' conveniently situated near the hall where assemblies and exams took place. After giving the space a thorough clean, I asked students to tell me what they wanted to have in their new prayer room. Of course, a prayer room was not exactly on their Christmas list but I did have a few respondents. 'A quiet place to relax,' was requested. Relaxation it was, then. Later that day, I found some large bean bags and scattered them around the room. 'Some art might be nice,' said one student. So I wrangled some soothing materials from our art department—landscape paintings, figural drawings and photographs of forest scenes. 'Candles!' was another request. Being health-and-safety conscious, I purchased some battery-powered candles and arranged them across a small table, which had a large white sheet draped over it to make it look like an altar. I made a colour photocopy of an icon of Jesus, stuck it to a cardboard backing and placed it on the table. One student recommended ordering some faux stained glass (plastic transparency) from Amazon, which I used to cover the small window of the room, allowing an ethereal, colourful light to enter when the sun shone. After a few days' work and a handful of students' ideas, it began to actually look like a chapel. Thus, my haphazard attempt at interior liturgical design.

...By Just Showing Up

The room saw no visitors in its first month. I set up prayer services, and a school counsellor would often meet students there for one-to-one conversations. Alas, no one used the space of their own volition, until one lunchtime when I stopped by to say prayers, and a student was sitting in the room on his own. He was a boy in Year 12, who had parked himself on a bean bag, lit a candle and was looking at the image of Jesus on the table. I went in and asked if he minded me sitting with him. We sat in silence for ten minutes until I finally asked his name. He told me who he was (for this reflection, I will name him Peter) and that he liked the new room. Peter was seventeen, good at drama and an excellent writer and poet. He was a deeply creative, thoughtful and imaginative teenager. He was also a transgendered student, transitioning from female to male, and had health issues which frequently caused him to be bedridden. His brother had been diagnosed as bipolar. Furthermore, aside from health difficulties, Peter's commute to school was long and he daily found himself exhausted by lunchtime. He had no specific faith tradition but used the room for long periods each day to 'have some space.' Over the next month, we began a series of conversations which became among the most treasured experiences from my time at the school.

One of the interesting and initially confusing aspects of my interaction with Peter was that, despite his circumstances—which I thought would occupy most of our conversations—we never once spoke about his sexuality, his gender, his brother or his home life. We spoke a little about his acting and writing but not in great detail. Most of the time we simply talked about stuff, what his day had been like and how he was feeling. Surprisingly, shortly before I left the school, he told me he had never felt able to speak to a 'religious person' before; that 'just being able to talk' meant everything; and he had even thought about God for the first time without realizing it. It was profoundly moving to hear these words, spoken by a brave student at a crucial time in his life. Yet I was also confused, in that the aspects of pastoral ministry I thought I was there for ended up being the least relevant. In the end, all I had needed to do was show up.

The One Who Calls You is Faithful...

In the following months, as exams loomed, Peter and many others started using the room more frequently. Word got around, it seemed. Students occasionally came for prayers, although more often they would crash on the bean bags during study periods, read together, light the candles and sit for hours, just dwelling in the space. Soon the room could not be used for services as so many students occupied it, and my conversations with Peter had to take place elsewhere. In his own unassuming and gentle way, Peter, like many students who used that room, helped me make sense not only of the purpose of the space, but the previous five years of ministry and many experiences since.

...And God Will Do This

One of the most pressing challenges in church schools is the need to make worship meaningful to increasingly diverse congregations, while maintaining integrity to a distinctly Christian vision. In the reflections that follow, I hope to articulate how experiences like the one recounted above might become opportunities to facilitate worship that allows young people in schools to embrace who they are, engage with questions which are important to them and, just maybe, acknowledge the God who created them in the first place.

In this book, I will draw on case studies which illustrate how Christian leaders might imaginatively incorporate students and staff of all faiths and none into worship, and help them to feel welcome to explore their spirituality and grow in faith and wisdom, both within and beyond their life in school.

The reflections are shaped around the eucharist, as my primary aim is to explore how eucharistic or sacramental worship in schools might be formational. The reason for this focus is two-fold. First, the eucharist is the pinnacle of Christian worship which provides the focal point for learning about Jesus' teaching and example. Secondly, in my experience, I have found that trying to maintain a faithful Christian witness in pluralistic contexts necessarily involves learning to understand how the sacraments confer sacred qualities to everyday life, even in a community which does not regularly celebrate them.

My aim in this book, then, is to explore a range of theological sources and practical illustrations which will provide a means for thinking about the meaning of the eucharist in schools. I will not be discussing in depth how to celebrate the eucharist in schools *per se*, as this is beyond the scope of this book and has been explored elsewhere.[2] Rather, I aim to offer clergy—but just as importantly, lay ministers, teachers and school leaders—examples of creative, interactive and participatory worship (both word-based and sensory) which might be utilized in either non-eucharistic or eucharistic liturgies. My intention is not to offer an instruction manual, but instead a theological reflection on myriad examples to encourage readers to reflect on their own experiences.

Gathering

This first chapter has been concerned with gathering: the first part of the liturgy where, be it in a church, chapel or even a simple prayer room, very different people can meet face to face. They could be friends or strangers. They could engage in actions as simple as lighting candles, or as complex as ancient traditions of the church. Either way, it is an opportunity for people to draw closer to one another and to God.

When I first met Peter, we both knew our experiences and perspectives were profoundly different. Yet, by taking time to simply gather and talk about things which did not reduce either of us to a preconception, we were able to discover one another's humanity afresh, and learn genuine hospitality and engagement from each other. That attitude permeated the atmosphere of that funny little room and made it holy. And even though such meetings are only the beginning of finding something much deeper and more complex, you will never know how much difference you have already made by just showing up.

Preparation 2

> I can't commit to something I don't think I can live up to.
>
> Emily, Norwich, 2005

Being Prepared to Listen

Once we have gathered, the next stage of the eucharist is preparation. Preparation for worship often comes in the form of confession, acknowledging self, neighbour and God. Serving in a school demands particular attentiveness in this respect. This second chapter will therefore articulate some theological principles for helping a school community prepare for worship.

Something I Cannot Live Up to...

Prior to ordination, I taught Religious Studies at a high school in North Norfolk. One day, in a class on Christian initiation, a student named Emily suddenly burst into tears and ran outside. When I later asked how she was, she said, 'I'm sorry sir...the whole "baptism-starting-again-thing" just sounded really nice.' I suddenly became nervous about how to deal with this vulnerable young person. Aside from being a new teacher dealing with a troubled student, I also found it difficult responding in light of my faith yet also being accountable to a school which did not endorse one particular faith. So I simply asked her, 'Why don't you ask your local church about it?' She responded, 'I can't commit to something I don't think I can live up to.'

Quite often, we allow our faith to become a barrier when in fact it demands radical hospitality. Emily had a degree of self-knowledge and integrity which gave her the confidence to ask difficult questions about faith, yet she was not equipped to work through these questions on her own. I thus had a student before me who was longing for some sort of guidance or even solidarity. However, despite my own confidence in my faith, I felt unprepared to navigate this situation within a secular institution—and in that moment my faith became a barrier to conversation, rather than a resource for healing.

Many children have the gift of being able to maintain integrity to who they are, while remaining open to asking questions of others. Part of what it means to be a Christian is to be hospitable, in a way that enables us to grow in conversation with others who might hold very different perspectives from our own. Even though the dynamic is different in a church school, given the increasingly broad demographic of our schools and the all-faiths-and-none agenda, many who work in church schools struggle with maintaining this exact balance. Yet, in the midst of church decline and increasing pluralism, the church has been making a concerted effort to balance a sincerely confessional, yet broad and hospitable, approach to spirituality, worship, governance and education itself.

The Importance of Attentiveness

The church's documentation on education published over the last several years has sought to articulate a distinctly Christian vision which is adaptable to the needs of diverse younger generations. Beginning with *The Church of England Vision for Education* (2016), leaders in this field have been working to develop a framework for building knowledge and skills in a modern church school by cultivating four particular virtues: wisdom, hope, community and dignity.[3] Such foundational principles outlined in this guidance have been developed further, particularly in the assessment criteria used to evaluate collective worship and religious education in Church of England schools. In the 2018 SIAMS inspection framework, for example, several categories—including vision and leadership, the impact of collective worship, and character development—place particular emphasis on balancing Christian identity with religious diversity.[4] The guidance specifically calls upon school leaders to 'embrace difference' and cultivate an ethos 'where all pupils, whatever their background or ability, can flourish because all are treated with dignity and respect.'[5] All of this seems to suggest that there is a positive move within church schools to encourage Christian hospitality in the midst of a pluralistic culture.

There is a positive move within church schools to encourage Christian hospitality

Perhaps more relevant to this study is the church's recent publication, *Spiritual Development: Interpretations of spiritual development in the classroom* (2019), which outlines a range of practices addressing student needs at formational stages, through experiential storytelling and 'sacred pathways.' Here, church school and Religious Education specialists describe 'an inclusive approach to spiritual development,' with the aim of helping students to become attentive to their own 'spiritual temperaments.' Through exercises which emphasize meditation, storytelling, experiential learning techniques and a range of worship styles, students are afforded the opportunity to engage, for example, as: sensates, traditionalists, ascetics, activists, caregivers, enthusiasts, intellectuals and / or contemplatives.[6] This kind of attentiveness to the tangible experiences of young people is a crucial starting point when engaging in school-based spiritual development. These narrative practices not only help us to see where God is in our midst, but also connect us to theological developments which are shaping the wider Christian community today.

The Importance of Narrative

Indeed, such developments seem to have their theological grounding in recent discourse on virtue and narrative within the field of Christian ethics—an area which has seen particular growth since the publication of Alasdair MacIntyre's seminal text, *After Virtue* (1981). MacIntyre's premise is that ethics is a matter of developing character over time within a community, which in turn develops the community's (and the individual's) capacity for moral decision-making.[7] Following on from this, today Christian ethicists and church leaders are increasingly attending to specific cultural narratives when formulating ethical theory, especially when it comes to cultivating virtue. Proponents of Christian virtue ethics argue that you cannot develop character or spiritual practice simply from historical analysis, *ad hoc* reflection or abstraction. Ethics must be grounded in real-life experience.

This has also led to a renewed interest in the relationship between narrative theology and the sacraments. Theologians such as Samuel Wells in *God's Companions* (2006) have written on how the sacraments of baptism and eucharist can become narratives and structures into which we weave our own experiences. The liturgy, like the Bible, is a story we perform, through which we learn practices that nurture virtue and shape our engagement with God and our communities.[8]

As we shall see later in this book, these narrative approaches are undoubtedly helpful in the context of school chaplaincy; however, it is also important to remember that the sacraments and the Bible are more than performed stories. Therefore, in addition to dwelling on story and structure, we are equally called to *participate in* a tangible, experiential reality which draws us closer to God and neighbour. And so it is worth briefly considering what makes sacraments distinctive.

Schools Shaped by the Eucharist

The eucharist is a sacrament, defined by St Augustine as 'an outward sign of an inward grace.'[9] There are two Protestant sacraments based on the example and commands of Christ: baptism and the eucharist. Among the many gifts which sacraments bestow is the gift of grace, which enables us to pursue Christian virtue—a gift especially associated with the eucharist.

The church therefore maintains that the eucharist (like baptism) is a distinctive act of Christian worship. However, as noted in the previous chapter, this book does not aim to rethink how we celebrate the eucharist within schools. Rather, my purpose is to suggest practices through which school communities—including those of all faiths and none—might perceive the sacramental or sacred in everyday experiences, thereby encouraging deeper spiritual engagement. As the theologians cited above remind us, we are able to encounter God in even the ordinary spheres of life. Therefore, while they are not sacraments, word-based and even sensory forms of worship can become sacramental or sacred. This reciprocally encourages school leaders and learners to think theologically about how the eucharist, for example, can inform every aspect of worship. It is the actual practice of such an ethos to which we now turn.

Words

3

> I ask for your thoughts…reflections…prayers…
> A high school student, New York, 2016

Using Words

The Liturgy of The Word refers to the first part of the eucharistic liturgy, where, after we have gathered and prepared for the service, we read Scripture, preach, teach and pray together, interweaving our own life stories into the narrative of Scripture and the purposes of God. In many respects, this part of the liturgy is about telling stories, bringing them to life by performing them in community. This third chapter will articulate some approaches for designing word-based liturgies, such as school assemblies and non-eucharistic worship. This is intended to be helpful for contexts which do not celebrate the eucharist, as well as offering examples for how to creatively approach the first part of the liturgy for schools that do. In both cases, I will also address inter-faith as well as other pluralistic contexts.

Choosing Words

Choosing what we say and how we say it, as mundane as this may seem, is one of the most complex things we do. What we say at the beginning of worship, therefore, is important.

One Monday morning, as was the weekly custom in my London school, all 1,300 students came into the large parish church which was their school chapel. Clearly, no one was feeling it. The teachers and I desperately tried getting the students to sing as the choir director undertook hymn practice. Yet barely any sound was heard—even the chapel choir was not awake. It was the start of the last week before autumn half-term and the students were exhausted as they staggered into church. No one wanted to be there.

My job at the start of assembly was to pray for the school, after which another department presented an assembly on the theme of the week, based on a combination of the department's own specialism, the liturgical calendar, commemorative events and world faith festivals. After the head teacher welcomed the school, the room fell silent for the prayer. As I stood before the crowd, despite having prepared some opening words, I realized that nothing

I could come up with was going to sound even remotely helpful, particularly as I saw one Year 7 girl in the front row roll her eyes almost into the back of her head. Then something occurred to me. I asked every person in the room to stretch…and then breathe deeply…and make the biggest yawn they could. Everyone started laughing. I told them that as they were so tired, they might as well stretch and yawn it out.

For three full minutes the room was full of teenagers (and teachers) groaning feverishly. As everyone groaned and creaked, I remembered that I had in my bag nearby a new prayer book I had been working on with students, which I was going to advertise during the assembly. I grabbed the book, and as the groans ended, I asked for silence. I opened the book and read the first prayer I saw, which was written by a girl in Year 10: 'God, today, you and I both know that there is nothing you and I can't face together. Amen.' You could have heard a pin drop. It was the students' words which were needed at that moment. Just using the mood in the room helped set the tone, and they listened because they were given the space to do so.

They listened because they were given the space to do so

Whose Words?

My experience has taught me that any act of worship, especially those taking place in schools, must be sincerely attentive to the very particular concerns of those gathered. A regular pattern of worship provides routine, structure and coherence, which is always helpful in school life. However, when the routine becomes dull, it is vital to ask the students what is important to them.

In the same week as previously mentioned, at my school in London, three girls from my recently completed confirmation class asked me if they could continue exploring their faith in school. We started a chapel team, where the students initiated everything from finishing the new prayer book and redesigning the school hymn book, to planning services, reading, preaching and serving at the altar. Other students became curious, especially when I stopped leading prayers at the front and the students led each week instead. When it came to designing the annual worship calendar and themes for the week, the students took the lead in liaising with the school community to survey what worked and what did not. They ran regular feedback on assemblies and eucharists so we could adjust the music, preaching and other interactive elements in order to make worship more accessible. Within three months, with minimal input from myself, the chapel team grew to twenty members, whilst the worship programme was almost entirely run by students.

Telling Stories

Although finding the right words is important, sometimes our words become occasions for action quite unintentionally (as above), and that is what grants us the opportunity to pause and discover something truly meaningful.

In one Church of England primary school in rural Norfolk, I was asked to take an assembly on the Parable of the Good Samaritan (Luke 10.25–37). During the assembly, I asked several Year 5 children to come to the front and act out the story as I read. Almost all of the volunteers, I later discovered, were children from the same, somewhat troubled (and well-known) family on a local estate. One girl asked to play the traveller and chose her best friend to be the robber. Her brothers asked to be the two passers-by, whilst the Samaritan was played by their cousin, a little girl in a wheelchair desperate for a part. The children simply made gestures at the front (they did not physically hit each other!), but as we walked through the story the children in the school hall suddenly became very aware of what was happening among their friends. Slowly, step by step, the robber pushed her friend to the ground, her brothers ignored her, and as the children paused to consider what was happening within this real family, the Samaritan wheeled over, invited the traveller to sit on her lap, then carried her across the hall.

Watching it unfold, the humorous yet somewhat serious action even took me by surprise. It was fascinating to see a familiar story come alive in a new way and, in the midst of the chaotic performance, to glimpse young people from a troubled context engaging with the narrative which was, in many respects, their own. After we prayed at the end, a teacher asked if we could do something on this topic again. A few weeks later, we started a series of RE classes on the theme, 'Who is my neighbour?' It was the pupils from the assembly who organized the first session.

Thoughts...Reflections...Prayers...

Even if not every moment of revelation is as unplanned as those above (although they often manifest that way), carefully and intentionally articulated space can and should be created within school worship. This ensures the congregation is empowered to engage on their own terms with communal, revelation-seeking activity. This is especially important in more pluralistic, particularly inter-faith, contexts.

I once visited an Episcopal school in New York which ended every school assembly with a set of intercessions planned by the student chapel team. To ensure there was space for all faiths and none, each petition for the needs of individuals, the community and the world, began with the words, 'I ask for your thoughts...reflections...prayers...' This was deliberate, so that each person in the room could engage in their own way, yet around a common purpose, petition and need, taking part as they were comfortable and able, through silence, space, then invitation—though this was never forced. There could be thoughts, maybe reflections, maybe even prayers, depending on how the individual felt they could participate.

In another Episcopal school in which I served (this time in Texas), each school division (clusters of year groups, such as Years 7–9, 10–11 and 12–13) would meet daily in the school chapel for a fifteen-minute prayer service or weekly eucharist. Following the pattern of Noonday Prayer in the American *Book of Common Prayer,* each service consisted of a greeting, psalm, reading, short homily, prayers, collect and blessing.[10] Six weeks into my first term, it was clear that the long-established pattern had grown old in one of our divisions. Students needed fewer words and more interaction. However, amidst their other commitments, the school worship band, chapel choir and drama groups could only find time to rehearse for occasional services. Therefore, I gathered my newly-formed student chapel team to ask what we could do.

One student said, 'We don't have enough time to pray and really think about the Scripture.' So, following a discussion about what they felt we needed in chapel, we cut the sermon completely and prayed through the Scripture instead. We developed a method akin to *Lectio Divina,* taking a Bible reading, breaking it into pieces, then adding petitions for particular intercessions throughout the text, connecting the needs of the community (which students identified) with the reading and its meaning.

After trying this a few times, the atmosphere in the chapel eventually changed from a recalcitrant huff to a more meditative peace. Eventually, although we kept our daily structure, the prayers through Scripture shaped the majority of the service. Students began gently speaking during the intercessions, offering their own petitions, even without being asked. Eventually the whole room was preaching and praying together as a community. Soon more students volunteered to come forward and actually preach or lead intercessions at the front—a pattern which became very helpful in another division the following year (see chapter six). In summary, the performance of words started to become an embodiment of what was really important to us.

4 Senses

> What should be done then, my friends? When you come together, each one has a hymn, a lesson, a revelation, a tongue, or an interpretation. Let all things be done for building up.
>
> 1 Cor 14.26

From Words to Senses

The fourth stage of the eucharistic liturgy centres on the sacrament itself: the Eucharistic Prayer and the sharing of communion and blessings. This is essentially where what we have shared and learned in the Liturgy of the Word can now become embodied and lived out in a more tangible and directly experiential way.

As I have already intimated, worship in school contexts of all faiths and none can and should be interactive, participatory, and sacramental. As a result, students can learn about the sacramentality or sacredness of everyday life, which could be formational as an act of worship in itself, or as part of the eucharistic service. What if generous attentiveness, like the involving enactment which ended the last chapter, resulted in curiosity about not only our personal stories, but in something beyond ourselves as we look to the altar?

Stimulating Senses

In my London school, the Remembrance eucharist was an annual worship highlight, marking an important moment in the life of school and nation. In 2014, the school sought to mark the 100th anniversary of the beginning of the First World War. The music, drama and dance departments all found themselves working on projects engaging with the theme. One senior teacher suggested we incorporate this material into the liturgy to add to our school's collective worship.

Alongside the usual tradition of processing, laying poppy wreaths and offering a solemn eucharist, we took a well-known modern mass setting, performed by our chapel choir, organist and school orchestra. The dance department created a liturgical dance responding to the mass setting: dancers, dressed in black, carried poppies and candles, moving through the building like soldiers through trenches. The 200-year-old church had multiple galleries and the dancers filled the entire building. Every time the mass setting came in, the dancers would file through the church, encouraging the congregation to look to the altar. The addition of war poetry, a dramatized gospel reading on the Beatitudes and a short homily from the chaplain, tied the elements together (Matt 5.3–12). Overall, we offered a service which taught—yet more importantly, embodied—the purpose of our gathering. It really seemed as though we were engaging with the historical events we were commemorating. And it felt as though we were moving towards the altar as a community, connecting with our neighbour and reaching out for something beyond, yet very much among, us.

In the words of St Paul, 'When you come together, each one has a hymn, a lesson, a revelation, a tongue, or an interpretation. Let all things be done for building up' (1 Cor 14.26). Such an act of worship, I believe, can help young people interpret biblical, historical, communal and spiritual narratives together and, in the process, cultivate virtue.

These activities can stand alone as a reflective act of worship or can become preparation for receiving the sacrament. Students could gain an awareness of the sacred space and of each other, of how they use their bodies in worship, or how they might live with intention. And, taking this a step further, by engaging in these kinds of narrative and sensory acts of worship, perhaps school communities can learn to appreciate what happens around the altar? Utilizing a more traditional church space with music, drama and dance enabled our diverse congregation to consider prayerfully what was happening in the liturgy, however they each interpreted this.

Perhaps school communities can appreciate what happens around the altar?

Sacred Space

Even the church building became an actor or story to engage with. In future years, we worked as a community to develop the Remembrance eucharist further. We connected the service to All Souls' Day and recalled other historical events which resonated with themes of grief, war and peace. One year, students read poetry remembering 9/11, based on recorded phone calls from loved ones from the planes as they approached the World Trade Centre.[11] Students pre-recorded the poetry through special effects to sound like distant answerphone messages, which echoed throughout the building, as we offered prayers for those whom we loved but saw no longer.

Another year, during the homily, we simply asked everyone to look up and consider the high windows of the church. During the Blitz, the church's windows had been blown out, with fragments collected by parishioners subsequently being added into the new windows. Meditating on local history and broken fragments (literally and figuratively), which had been reconnected in the presence of God, provided our community with another way into praying at the eucharist. As we later broke and shared the bread, we were able to think in more depth about how, despite the brokenness of our world, we were still one body.

Common Sense

Interestingly, storytelling can utilize drama, dance, music and student creativity—even the building itself—which are often overlooked elements when it comes to embodying worship in schools. Perhaps this is partly because we rarely take the time simply to look around us and appreciate the gifts of the people and the location we are in. School life always moves fast, and nurturing a meditative culture is one of the greatest gifts the church can give to the institution.

In one voluntary-controlled primary school in Norfolk, the student council and parent-teacher association raised money for new windows for the school hall. Two high windows were painted by students on stained glass, under the guidance of a local artist. Each displayed a large tree surrounded by animals, light, leaves and other symbols of nature, during spring and autumn respectively. Once the windows were installed, we held a Harvest Festival service in the hall for students, teachers and families, offering Scripture readings, poems, harvest hymns and songs. During the service, I poured some water and salt into a small bowl, prayed a blessing, then two students took rosemary sprigs and sprinkled the windows (and most of the congregation) as we prayed God's blessing on the community.

Although this particular act of worship was not held in the context of the eucharist, I found myself reflecting on how this was an occasion for real thanksgiving. Harvest, like the term 'eucharist,' is about thanksgiving, which is what we were doing in that hall, sharing in a creative, artistic, common project which connected children, parents and staff to each other, as well as to the local community. And then, through a playful, sensory, even childlike act of worship, we facilitated a valuable opportunity to look around us, physically interacting with, and celebrating how, God had blessed us in our school.

Sensory Worship

As with the eucharist itself, engaging the senses is vital in any act of worship, and this is especially important if you do not have access to a church or chapel. In London, I had the privilege of being the first chaplain at the Church of England's first and only free school for special educational needs (SEN).

This satellite school was born out of our well-established mainstream school, as a response to the particular needs of an inner-city London community. The school offered a co-educational programme for students aged 11–16, all of whom experienced some form of autism or speech, language, communication and/or behavioural needs, as well as, for some, physical disabilities. The student population was approximately 70% Muslim, 20% different faiths and no faith, and 10% Christian.

It is vital for ministers to seek collaboration with their fellow staff and students

This was a challenging context. In such conditions, as always, it is vital for ministers to seek collaboration with their fellow staff and students. Over five years, I spent considerable time working with specialist teachers and speech, language and behaviour therapists, designing a worship programme which would work accessibly and compassionately with the particular students we served. Since we had no chapel, we had to establish a comfortable worship space in the hall, carefully mapping out how students would sit, kneel, stand and move. Then we designed services employing techniques already used in classroom teaching and therapy sessions. Every service was formatted on PowerPoint, utilizing word maps, sign language and SEN and Makaton symbol systems to teach new words, break down Scripture readings and guide students through prayers—including the eucharist, which followed a simplified form.[12]

In worship, we also applied regulatory breathing techniques and storytelling methods, commonly used for processing emotions after difficult experiences. We guided students through intercessions and provided space for silence, which afforded opportunities to reflect. This also allowed those of different faiths to engage in their own spirituality, even within a distinctively Christian liturgy. We incorporated dramatized Scripture readings (often videos of students acting), as well as music, dance and other sensory elements into our homilies, which were frequently led by students from the school's main site (see chapter five).

Senses, Sacraments and Technology

During another eucharist at the school, we retold Mark's account of Jesus' baptism and his calling of the first disciples by the sea (Mark 1.1–11). The reading appeared in simplified form on the screen accompanied by SEN symbols, as I placed a glass bowl and water jug on a pedestal in the centre of the room. As student helpers from the mainstream school slowly narrated the story, a pupil from the special school would walk over, pour water into the bowl, gently move their hands through the water with a sea shell, drop in a paper cross with a handwritten prayer, then light a candle and place it next to the bowl. Others then came forward, touched the water, lit a candle and offered a prayer, before kneeling again in silence, after which we moved into a set of intercessions based on the reading, followed by the Eucharistic Prayer.

Whether students received communion or a blessing, or simply knelt in silence, every person in the room was engaged; their behaviour was calm and their body language measured. Everyone seemed attentive to the fact that something significant was happening—and most importantly, everyone had a place.

Such interactive elements became key within the structure of our carefully articulated weekly worship. Each week began with a morning assembly following set themes of the week (see chapters three and five). Then, to provide daily collective worship, I prepared a PowerPoint-based meditation which teachers guided students through on their classroom smartboard during registration at the end of each day, to calm students before they left for home. This involved a period of silence, then a reminder of the week's assembly, followed by a sensory activity based on the theme of the week, and finally a silent meditation on a Bible verse and a prayer. Over time, with increasing student and teacher input, we developed a pattern of worship which worked for a profoundly diverse and vulnerable population of children, providing a place of genuine hospitality, inclusion and participation. Gradually, this hospitality became a pattern for living beyond the hall.

5

Blessings

> Do not be conformed to this world, but be transformed by the renewing of your minds.
>
> Rom 12.2

Sharing a Blessing

After the sacrament comes the Blessing and Dismissal, where the congregation go out into the world to share what they have learned and to be a sign of blessing to others. This chapter therefore explores how integrated, participatory school worship might empower students to go and live what they have learned in worship, whoever and wherever they may be. If we can facilitate acts of worship in our schools which truly transform minds and hearts, where students are able to lead in worship, perhaps they will consider for themselves how they might serve one another and God both within and beyond their school communities.

Becoming a Blessing

At the special school, following the worship programme outlined in the previous chapter, the students initiated a council and chapel team, where the children held their own forum to discuss issues which they felt were important in their school. Students would give feedback on worship, nominating themes and festivals from world faiths and even charitable causes, which they could reflect upon in worship and then contribute to in wider school life.

We eventually began holding assemblies themed around initiatives such as National Mental Health Awareness Week and National Anti-Bullying Week. This worship pattern was mirrored at the mainstream school, where students and teachers equally recognized the importance of engaging with such issues. At the mainstream site's first assembly on mental health, some students from the special school took part so they could introduce themselves to the rest of the community and raise awareness of their contexts. Afterwards, my chapel team and several Sixth Formers met the students, and they became interested in what was happening at the special school. At the students' suggestion, we started a peer-mentoring scheme, where older students could carry out their work experience at the special-school site. This helped mainstream students learn compassion and new technical skills, while also creating connections between the two campuses, so that the special school felt more included and involved in wider community life. Eventually, the chapel team began assisting me with services at the special school by rehearsing readers, choosing readings, planning the PowerPoints and teaching sensory homilies to the younger children.

Worship at both schools soon began engaging with a range of issues relevant to our young people: from reaching out to marginalized groups—such as LGBTQ+ students, minority races and religions—to asking questions related to special needs and disability. It was fascinating to see how this culture developed out of the collaborations which had evolved around our chapel programme.

At the main site, quite often an assembly was presented by an independently initiated student group (overseen by a teacher), who would offer a range of different perspectives on a particular issue. Such assemblies would raise students' awareness of important social concerns and they would be interested in continuing the conversation. Eventually, some students established small societies (under the supervision of an interested member of staff), which empowered them to organize their own community conversations around important emotional health issues, as well as to support one another in practical and immediate ways.

Overcoming Barriers to Blessing

Of course, this was not always smooth sailing. Despite having established a healthy and vital relationship with senior leaders over several years, for pastoral reasons a number of my colleagues were concerned for students' well-being in the midst of such vulnerable, challenging situations, and initially withheld support for certain chapel activities which were deemed controversial.

It is moments like these that prompt serious pause for thought: when you find yourself discerning how to exercise what you believe will be a fruitful ministry, imaginatively working with others to overcome the limits of an institution.

Some questioned if we should be exploring provocative issues from a faith perspective

At this point in the chapter, and the book, it may seem as though my service among young people has been a constant stream of joy and wonder. But chaplaincy is not easy. Some of the school's staff questioned if we should be exploring provocative issues from a faith perspective, or if we were giving too much responsibility to vulnerable students, or if we should even teach the eucharist in such an obvious way to a profoundly diverse school. Their reasons for this ranged from fear of proselytization or exposure to sensitive material, to overburdening students. Whilst understanding many of these concerns, I insisted that we should allow the students to make the call on this, otherwise they would never truly own the agenda.

Thanks to a highly collaborative head teacher, my chapel team was invited to make a presentation to the governors on how they perceived the worship programme and students' roles within it. To my delight, and with barely any input from me, the students rose to the challenge. It was fascinating and moving to witness pupils openly discussing their faith before a panel of adults, demonstrating that they were capable of representing, and making decisions for, their peers. They asked questions, tested ideas and by the end you could not really say no. By not simply telling them what to think, we had provided a space for the students to develop their own relationship with God and their own ministry.

Sometimes pastoral ministry is about facilitating opportunities for people to discover faith

Sometimes pastoral ministry is less about telling people where to find God, and more about facilitating opportunities for them to discover faith on their own terms. All you have to do is 'show up' and ask the obvious question, 'What's important to you?,' then learn to wait for the answer. This, interestingly, is where parishes, not simply school chaplaincies alone, have a profound strength.

In School, Church and World

During the second year of my curacy in North Norfolk, a nationwide Christian youth-work initiative had started a new branch in our area and were looking for parishes with which to partner. Having recently established a parish youth group, I welcomed the opportunity to join different churches in the district in this ecumenical effort to share resources and connect young people in our community.

Our small youth group was formed of children from our Church of England primary schools, who embraced the idea of meeting more young people from beyond the parish. The wider youth initiative quickly developed a series of weekly after-school clubs, which took place in our local primary and high schools. Despite not all being church schools, each institution was enthusiastic about the opportunity to partner with community action groups to support families. Most of the children who attended were looking for something to do when, for various reasons, they did not want to return home too soon at the end of the day.

As conversations among both churched and non-churchgoing children developed, it soon materialized that, as well as games and food, what was equally missing in their lives was a deeper sense of purpose. This was true even among our parish youth group, who had become bored with a pattern of worship and community engagement that did not speak to them. One evening, a group of students walked past me as I was entering a community hub for people with learning disabilities. As they passed by, the students asked me what went on in there. After sparking some curiosity by telling them what the centre was for, one of the students said, 'I've never met anyone like that before.'

During Holy Week the following year, our group of ecumenical partners in the town organized a social action week. Each day, every church youth group and those who attended the school clubs would meet at one of our churches. In the morning, we played games, held group discussions and organized a student-led act of worship, followed by lunch. In the afternoon, we would split off into groups for social action projects in the local community—from painting fences and gardening, to helping with care home visits and services, including within the community hub where my students had seen me.

It was fascinating to witness some of our most disillusioned young people experiencing real joy at the opportunity to offer something so simple, yet so valuable, to someone else. One afternoon, I found myself leaving the community hub with a group of students, including the one whose question first sparked the idea for this project. When I asked them, 'How you do you think this afternoon went?' the student replied, 'I used to think people like that were weird, but all they want is what I want.' And, as we reached the church where parents were arriving to collect the teenagers, the student turned and said, 'Are we going there again?'

The joyful combination of worship, service and community connections in preparation for Easter was about as formational as you could get.[13] What is more, the common effort did not end there. A few weeks after Easter, our young people expressed a continued interest in meeting, worshipping and serving together. We started running meetings with service opportunities on a termly basis, coinciding with long school holidays and Christian festivals.

Ministry in schools is not just about school chaplains; church ministers have a role to play, too. This project became a blessing to the community because different organizations collaborated around a common purpose. The church truly became the body of Christ within the community—and all of this was possible, not because we told our young people what to do, but because we empowered them as Christian leaders.

6

Starting Again

This final reflection will not begin with an explanation, a quotation or a specific aspect of the liturgy. Rather, it will begin as every school worship programme must—completely from scratch.

An Invitation

At the beginning of my second year serving an Episcopal school in Texas, one of our student year groups was not participating as much in worship as they had previously. The strategy of holding daily Prayer Book-based assemblies and a weekly eucharist (outlined in chapter three) was not working. Volunteers started to dwindle, people stopped singing during services and even during the eucharist behaviour was poor. After talking with different teachers, I discovered that there were several presenting issues and that, for some time, there had been a combination of student discipline problems and general fatigue among staff.

Then one day, after a particularly difficult morning, none of the assigned student readers came to the front of the chapel. Neither students nor teachers were paying attention. Spontaneously I introduced a time of silence, and we spent ten minutes simply dwelling in each other's presence. At the end of our allotted time, I prayed for us. Before everyone was dismissed, I announced that things seemed difficult in the chapel at the moment and that I wanted to do something that would be helpful for everyone. The next day, therefore, I would organize readings and prayers, but would leave them at the back of the chapel. If people wanted Scripture and prayers then they could volunteer to read them, but if they needed silence, we would have silence instead.

The next day, I placed four sheets of paper on the ground at the chapel entrance: a greeting, a Bible reading, some prayers and a collect. As the congregation came in, I sat in the pews. No one volunteered to read and so we had silence. Although it was awkward at first, students soon stopped picking at their clothes, whilst teachers stopped staring out of the window and began looking at each other. After a while, it was good for us just to be in the same room with no one making any demands. This continued for several days. We even stopped celebrating the eucharist, to allow similar time for silence. I asked the head of year if she was happy with this and she told me she felt as though some space could be what we needed.

The following Friday, as the children came in, three boys noticed the readings on the ground. 'When do I read this?' asked one of them. I told them when to read and where to stand. The boys, none of whom had read in chapel before, went to the lectern and, without any cues, led the assembly. There were initial awkward stutters, girls giggled and teachers were fearful given who these particular boys were. But they gave the readings, offered the prayers and even shared a blessing. And at the end, I thanked them and we were dismissed.

Building Bridges

Over the next few weeks, each day I would leave the readings on the ground and, later, on the altar. Students would come in, unrehearsed, take the reading they felt comfortable with, then lead from the front. Some days, prayer would begin in silence, readers would sit at the back or among friends, and a microphone would go around to each speaker. This way, we could look to the altar and pray to God together. After a while, they would begin improvising with the prayers, offering the names of those they wanted to mention as they prayed. We thus began a daily prayer list, compiled by students and monitored by the chapel team.

Students started asking about the meaning of the readings after services. So, we started a game called 'Thirty-second Preacher.' After the reading, students would silently reflect on what they had heard, then volunteers would offer a thirty-second reflection on the reading, followed by a prayer for someone special to them or a word of advice to their peers. Soon, some students asked if they could learn how to preach and pray in public more. We began using the *Lectio Divina* method which I had used elsewhere in school (see chapter three). During one lunchtime chapel meeting, a group of interested students gathered and followed the method, praying with the readings, then constructing homilies and intercessions, which they offered in chapel the following week.

Building the Liturgy

As we were building trust and confidence, we also built services in the same way—from scratch. We reintroduced the eucharist. One day, the chapel team and I sat among the congregation without wearing robes. As the service started, we stood and slowly walked to the sanctuary in silence. We gathered around the altar and, after a short Liturgy of the Word, we celebrated the eucharist: we had no robes (other than a stole I wore), no ceremony, no music. The congregation's behaviour was respectful, the participation good (strong voices throughout) and at the end the servers and I returned to our places in the pews. Everyone in the room sat for five minutes in silence. Something had changed.

The next week, we did the same thing, except when we came to the sermon. Instead of preaching, I invited everyone to walk around the chapel and explore the building. After ten minutes, we had a Question and Answer on different things they had found in the chapel and what they meant. We started talking about the eucharist and its meaning. Since we were running out of time, and services were always in the middle of the day, we said grace instead of celebrating the eucharist before going to lunch. Soon we started saying grace at the end of every assembly before lunch. This, in turn, led to further conversations about what the eucharist meant.

Learning to be Thankful

Later that term, we held an assembly where students and teachers took a piece of paper and wrote one question they felt they could never have previously asked about faith, the Bible, the eucharist or whatever was on their mind. I collected the answers and these formed the basis for the chapel programme for the rest of the academic year. Every service was based on a theme or question raised by a student or teacher. Over a number of weeks, from the congregation's input, we reintroduced music (led by students and staff), started planning services together (which the chapel team oversaw), and reintroduced the more ceremonial elements of the eucharist. And whenever we felt as though things were difficult again, or we just needed a change, we would have a stripped-back eucharist, a silent service or incorporate more student-driven elements, so that distractions could be limited and the prayers of the congregation could come to the fore.

Eventually, the chapel and the altar itself became a place where people felt comfortable. It seemed as though, rather than simply being a routine, worship had become a celebration again, in which our community gathered together around a common table, with a common purpose. The chapel became a place where students and teachers would share what was important to them, as much as having chaplain-led worship. Their concerns, interests, passions and fears became the subjects of our preaching and prayer. Worship became a space where community service was talked about; where students and teachers would discuss elements of what they were doing in wider school life and in the classroom; and we would pray about them. Although life in school is never perfect, I think we came far.

Engaging the Student Voice

In many ways, what we shared in that chapel brought home two key elements which I believe can help shape the development of creative worship in any school.

First, we must remember that the term 'eucharist' means 'thanksgiving.' So many of the examples we have considered ultimately beg that one essential question: 'What are you thankful for?' Engaging staff and students with this question is surely a healthy starting point for developing any act of school worship.

And finally, Jesus took time to be with people and waited until they were ready to respond. Sometimes, the answer is not so much an exciting programme but a willingness to simply be present. You will never know what difference you make by just showing up.

Notes

1 All Bible quotations are taken from *The Holy Bible—New Revised Standard Version*, Anglicized Edition (Oxford University Press, 1995).

2 J Brooke, *Holy Communion in Primary Schools* (Grove Education booklet eD41) is an example from Grove which explores this theme.

3 Church of England, *Church of England Vision for Education: Deeply Christian, Serving the Common Good* (London: Church House Publishing, 2016) especially pp 1–2.

4 The Church of England Education Office and The Methodist Church, Statutory Inspection of Anglican and Methodist Schools (SIAMS): *An Evaluation Schedule for Schools and Inspectors* (London: The Church of England Education Office, 2018).

5 SIAMS: *An Evaluation Schedule for Schools and Inspectors, op cit,* particularly p 11.

6 D Holloway, A Lumb, L Mills, A Rickett, S Vickery, T Wilson, K Wright, N Genders, *Spiritual Development: Interpretations of Spiritual Development in the Classroom* (London: The Church of England Education Office, 2019) especially K Wright, 'Sacred Pathways,' pp 27–31.

7 A MacIntyre, *After Virtue—A Study in Moral Theory*, Third Edition (Notre Dame, IN: University of Notre Dame Press, 2007).

8 S Wells, *God's Companions—Reimagining Christian Ethics* (Oxford: Blackwell, 2006).

9 St Augustine of Hippo, *The City of God,* H Bettenson (trans) (London: Penguin Classics, 1984) pp 377–379 (Book X, Chapter V).

10 Protestant Episcopal Church, *The Book of Common Prayer and Administration of the Sacraments and Other Rites and Ceremonies of the Church Together with The Psalter or Psalms of David, According to the Use of the Episcopal Church* (New York: Church Publishing Inc, 1979) especially pp 103–107.

11 M Symmons Roberts, 'Last Words,' from *The Half Healed* (London: Jonathan Cape, 2008).

12 Church of England, *Additional Eucharist Prayers—With Guidance on Celebrating the Eucharist with Children* (London: Church House Publishing, 2012).

13 E Howatt, *Igniting Potential: Developing Character and Leadership Through Social Action* (Grove Education booklet eD39) also explores this theme.